Spinosaurus

Written by David White
Illustrated by Pam Mara

Library of Congress Cataloging-in-Publication Data

White, David, 1952–
  Spinosaurus.

  (Dinosaur library)
  Summary: Describes the characteristics of this meat-eating dinosaur that lived in North Africa during the Cretaceous Period.
  1. Spinosaurus—Juvenile literature. 2. Dinosaurs—Juvenile literature. [1. Spinosaurus. 2. Dinosaurs]
  I. Title. II. Series.
  QE862.S3W48 1988   567.9'7   87-36914
  ISBN 0-86592-517-8

Rourke Enterprises, Inc.
Vero Beach, FL 32964

Quetzalcoatlus

Parasaurolphus

Deinosuchus

Corythasaurus

Spinosaurus

Oviraptor

Spinosaurus

Pachycephalosaurus

Anatosaurus

Struthiomimus

Scolosaurus

Rutiodon

Psittacosaurus

The dawn arrived suddenly at the edge of the desert. One minute, the plains were cloaked in darkness. The next, they shimmered in the harsh subtropical sun.

Although the sun was above the horizon, the air was still chilly with night. In the shadows cast by a rocky outcrop, Spinosaurus and his mate woke and stirred themselves.

Slowly, Spinosaurus raised himself from the squatting position in which he had slept, until he stood on all four limbs. He knew that he must get warm quickly. Once his blood was warm, he could move fast – faster than the creatures whose blood was still cold.

Spinosaurus emerged from the shadows into the sunlight and looked around him. Then, purposefully, he turned his body until one side was facing the sun. This was so that the sun's rays could heat the blood circulating through the great sail on his back.

Spinosaurus felt the warmth coursing through his veins. His limbs loosened and his brain became more alert. Soon, he was ready to hunt for his prey.

He moved off across the plain, his lowered head swinging from side to side. He was searching for tracks in the sand. Soon he found what he was looking for. There were three pairs of tracks, left by large, three-toed creatures. The hunt was on.

Spinosaurus found his prey on the broad plain of the river. Three Ouranosauruses were feeding on the vegetation which grew near the river. They stood on their broad hind limbs, tearing at the plants which grew in the crevices of the rocks.

Scenting Spinosaurus in the wind, they lowered themselves onto all fours and began to lumber away from the danger. Spinosaurus gave chase.

However, the Ouranosauruses were not easy prey, for they could run as fast as Spinosaurus. This was because their blood, too, had been warmed in the sails on their backs.

Yet Spinosaurus was able to keep up with the Ouranosauruses. He would have caught one of them but they suddenly split up. As each Ouranosaurus ran off in a different direction, Spinosaurus hesitated. Which one should he pursue.

His hesitation allowed the Ouranosauruses to escape. Spinosaurus halted and watched them go. Slowly he returned to the banks of the river. If he could not eat, he could at least drink. He drank warily, watching for the giant crocodiles that inhabited the riverbank. These enormous animals would lie in wait for dinosaurs who came to drink at the river.

Spinosaurus returned to the open plain. In the distance, he could see a great cloud of dust. This was a clear signal that a herd of Sauropods was on the move.

As Spinosaurus approached the herd, he could see that it was a large one. Some 20 to 30 Brachiosaurus were making their slow way across the plain. The adults stayed on the outside of the herd, while the young were kept inside. This was to give them protection from attack.

Spinosaurus was interested only in the young Brachiosauruses. However, the adults made a defensive wall with their bodies, so that it was impossible for him to reach them. Spinosaurus angrily snapped and tore at their massive legs, but to no avail.

Finally, he turned away in frustration. Spinosaurus was tired and dusty and hot. The sun was now high in the sky. There was no shade on the plain, so Spinosaurus turned towards the sun, so that the sun's rays did not strike his sail head-on. When he was cooler, he continued the hunt. He saw flying reptiles circling in the distance – a sign that some large creature had died. As he approached, he saw it was the carcass of Titanosaurus, a sauropod.

Several Quetzalcoatluses were perched on the
carcass, tearing at the flesh. Spinosaurus chased them
away. He was hungry, and he eagerly began to eat. But
his meal was interrupted by a roar. Tyrannosaurus,
too, had seen the flying reptiles and had come to feed on
the carcass. Now it was Spinosaurus's turn to be chased
away.

Spinosaurus was no match for Tyrannosaurus. Besides, a fight could damage the precious sail on his back.

Disappointed and still hungry, Spinosaurus returned to the river bank. His arrival surprised Gallimimus, who was foraging for insects and lizards. The hunter lunged at his prey, but Gallimimus was too fast. As Spinosaurus's jaw snapped shut, the creature sprang away, disappearing into the foliage.

Spinosaurus decided to rejoin his mate on the higher ground. Together, they moved across the plain in the heat of the afternoon, ever watchful. Eventually, they found what they were looking for – the undisturbed carcass of a Parrosaurus. The animal had been killed by a Tyrannosaurus when it became separated from the herd. The Tyrannosaurus had eaten its fill, and left the rest to the scavengers of the plain.

Spinosaurus and his mate ate eagerly. This time they could eat as much as they wanted without being disturbed.

As the shadows lengthened, Spinosaurus and his mate returned to the rocky ledge. The evening was cool after the intense heat of the day. Spinosaurus settled down to sleep.

Spinosaurus and the Cretaceous World

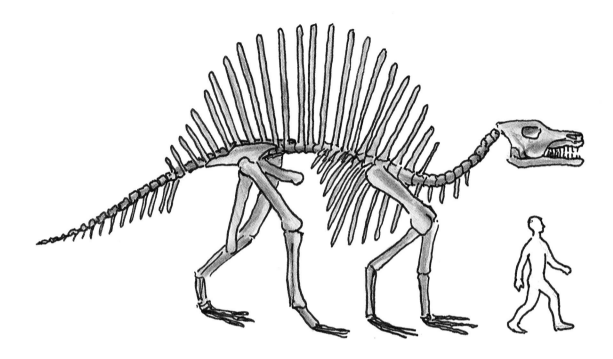

A speculative skeleton of Spinosaurus compared in size to a man.

The time of Spinosaurus

The Mesozoic Era, or the "age of dinosaurs" as it is sometimes known, was between 225 million years ago and 65 million years ago. Geologists divide the era into three periods: the Triassic, the Jurassic and the Cretaceous.

The first two periods are much shorter than the third. The Cretaceous Period lasted for 71 million years. Spinosaurus lived at some time during this period.

The land of Spinosaurus

In the Cretaceous Period, the continents separated and acquired something like the shape they have today. The continent of Africa separated from Europe and Asia.

Spinosaurus lived in North Africa. Fossils have been found in Egypt, which is why palaeontologists have called it *Spinosaurus aegypticus*. The climate of North Africa was then subtropical and more moist than it is today.

The family tree of Spinosaurus

Spinosaurus belonged to the carnosaur family. Carnosaurs evolved in the Triassic Period. They soon achieved large sizes. Teratosaurus, who lived 200 million years ago, was 20 feet long. In the Jurassic Period, carnosaurs like Megalosaurus (the first dinosaur to have been discovered in 1822) and Allosaurus appeared. This branch of the family developed into the fearsome Tyrannosaurus in the Cretaceous Period.

Another branch resulted in Spinosaurus. Spinosaurus is an interesting example of how a carnosaur adapted to climatic conditions. Most carnosaurs lived in forests, swamps and jungles. Spinosaurus lived on the edge of the desert. It evolved its sail to cope with the intense heat, just as Dimetrodon did in the Permian Period.

Other meat eaters

Spinosaurus had many meat-eating

competitors. Chief among them was his carnosaur cousin, Tyrannosaurus. But there were others, like the enormous Quetzalcoatlus. This was a pterosaur, and probably the largest flying creature that ever lived. The creature had a wingspan of 39 feet and weighted over 180 pounds. It scavenged for food, feeding on the bodies of dead dinosaurs.

Plant eaters

Once the southern continents, like Africa, had separated from the northern continents, the dinosaurs were no longer free to move throughout the world. This meant that dinosaurs evolved differently in different parts of the world.

In the northern continents, like North America, a new generation of highly successful plant eaters evolved – the hadrosaurs, the ankylosaurs and the ceratopsians. However, these same types never evolved in the southern continents such as Africa. In these continents, plant eaters continued to be slow-moving, slow-witted sauropods like Brachiosaurus and Parrosaurus. They were easy prey for the meat-eaters.

Some plant eaters, did evolve that were able to escape from carnosaurs. One of these is Ouranosaur.

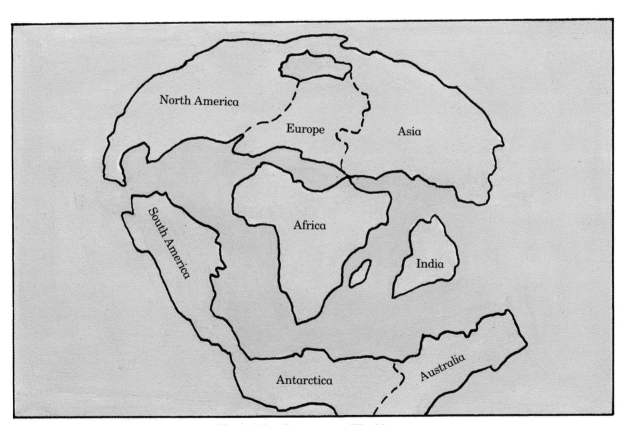

Map of the Cretaceous World